LIFE
LEADERSHIP
&LEGACY

101 TIPS
FOR EMERGING JUSTICE LEADERS

FORWARD BY DR. AMANDA COLEMAN-MASON

SECOND EDITION

Resmaa Menakem & June Davidson

Printed in the United States of America

ISBNs: 978-0-9984248-2-8 (paperback)
        978-0-9984248-3-5 (ebook)

Cover by: DADEZINER AT FIVERR.COM

Book design by: Patti Frazee at pattifrazee.com

Self-study design by: Resmaa Menakem, The Cultural
Wellness Center, Minneapolis, Minnesota

Black House Publishings
7400 Metro Blvd. Suite 224
Edina, MN 55439
www.blackhousepublishings.com

Testimonials

Resmaa Menakem, President of Justice Leadership Solutions, was my first coach. I did not know what to expect. He put me at ease by speaking with me in calm tones, asking questions that made me think, and guiding me to make decisions. I appreciate Resmaa's patience, guidance, and knowledge. I gladly recommend his services because he keeps his clients focused on their goals and their results.

– Brenda Gayle Bryant
the Gayle group, www.thegaylegroup.com
author of *FSL–Finance as a Second Language*

I would not hesitate to recommend Resmaa to any group or individual that is seeking a thorough, research-based, group facilitation process. It is with great honor and void any hesitation that I endorse Resmaa Menakem for any person or group seeking in-depth and knowledgeable training and facilitation on some meaningful and relevant topics.

– Corey Yeager, MA, LMFT
Educational Equity Coordinator,
Office of Black Male Student Achievement
Minneapolis Public Schools

Resmaa's motivating and accountability coaching skills helped me to stay focused on my goals. He was consistent in practicing a "can do" attitude and in his ability to inspire and motivate me in keeping my mission and direction in the forefront. I wholeheartedly recommend Resmaa Menakem as a coach to anyone whose intention is to grow or improve any situation, personally or professionally.

– Amanda Coleman-Mason, Ph.D.
CEO Adissa Transnational Leadership Coaching
Author of *Customer Service Excellence for Police: 101 Tips on Policing in Cross-Cultural Communities*

I have experienced Resmaa Menakem, President of Justice Leadership Solutions, as a skillful trainer. As a trainer, he has a knack for making complex material relatable and exciting. He makes a connection with audience members almost immediately and presents information in a way that is compatible with a variety of learning styles. The Psychological First Aid training I did with him was not only interesting and applicable to my work but I also feel like I gained an important life skill that I have used countless times since then.

— Katherine Bisanz, MSW, LGSW

I have observed and participated in workshops/classes facilitated by Resmaa Menakem of Justice Leadership Solutions and have found his connection with participants to be superior and very sensitive. He demonstrates a very knowledgeable understanding of trauma, and especially historical trauma. His training on Psychological First Aid is efficient, and he ensures that participants are prepared to understand the physiological impact of trauma as well as the impact of historical racism. I highly recommend his training and group facilitation as well as his courses on Psychological First Aid.

— Stella Whitney-West, MBA
CEO NorthPoint Health & Wellness Center
Minneapolis

Resmaa Menakem, founder of the Justice Leadership Solutions training program in Minneapolis, taught the first backbone of community activists as psychological first aid responders…with a grounded depth that drew us to his wisdom and insight that prepared us for the future traumas he knew would come.

Resmaa knew, and taught us how to lessen and heal the impact of trauma at its source. Together, we create one less wound, and more strength, that gets passed along.

— Ashley Satorius
Community member, Social justice activist
Minneapolis

Resmaa Menakem, LICSW is a captivating teacher, facilitator, and presenter. The trifecta embodied by his passion, knowledge and life experience with trauma are unmatched. His training as a mental health therapist further aids his ability to engage the audience in an empathic and therapeutic manner. Mr. Menakem's cross-cultural experiences abroad make him an ideal candidate for working with a diverse range of people. It is both a pleasure and honor to recommend him to those looking for training or consultation services. You will not be disappointed.

– Larry G. Tucker, LMFT
CEO & President
Kente Circle, LLC

Resmaa Menakem, President of Justice Leadership Solutions, was a first-rate master coach. I have been law enforcement professional and international trainer for twenty-plus years; Resmaa has given me some of the best coachings I have ever had. I have had previous experiences with coaches and found the relationships not very satisfying. Resmaa spoke with me in calm tones, asked questions, encouraged me to think about leadership courage and justice in ways that I had not. Resmaa did this while holding me accountable to my stated plans even through my professional struggles. I unequivocally recommend Resmaa's services because he keeps his clients focused on their life, leadership, and justice legacy goals.

– Christopher S Mason
Ph.D. Public Policy (ABD)

Acknowledging Our Ancestors

On this soil, trauma has taken earlier path: one that spread from the bodies of European colonists to the bodies of Native people by genocide, and then through many generations of their descendants.

An estimated 18 million Native people were custodians of this land when colonized European arrived. Native people and their ancestors had lived here for an estimated 14,000 years.

Today this land contains over 204 million white Americans, over 46 million Black Americans, and just over five million Native Americans. The unique arc of trauma in the Native American body is a story that is only now beginning to be told.

I offer my respect and acknowledgment to the people who were stewards of this land long before people from Africa and Europe first came here.

LIFE
LEADERSHIP
&LEGACY

101 TIPS

FOR EMERGING JUSTICE LEADERS

FORWARD BY DR. AMANDA COLEMAN-MASON

SECOND EDITION

Resmaa Menakem & June Davidson

but Resmaa Menakem occupies the role as a master of critical thinking when it comes to integrating and balancing life, promoting leadership, and creating a prideful legacy. Everyone whose passion is to serve their community and to be the best in who they are should read this book.

– Dr. Amanda Coleman-Mason, Ph.D.
Transnational Justice Leadership Coach;
CEO of Adissa Justice Leadership Coaching;
Author of *Customer Service Excellence for Police: 101 Tips on Policing in Cross-Cultural Communities*

Introduction

Author Introduction

Resmaa Menakem is the founder of Justice Leadership Solutions. He is an accomplished author of three compelling books: *101 Tips for Emerging Justice Leaders*, *My Grandmothers Hands: Racialized Trauma and the Pathways to Mending Our Hearts and Bodies*, and an authoritative book on conflict in relationships titled *Rock the Boat: How to Use Conflict to Heal and Deepen Relationships*.

Resmaa is a world-class Justice Leadership coach, entrepreneur, mediator, and certified SEP trauma therapist. Resmaa served as a community care counselor in Afghanistan with his brother, who is a police officer from Dallas. Resmaa Menakem has been a guest on *Oprah* and *Dr. Phil* as a subject matter expert and Clinical Director for DV Treatment, and has also been the behavioral health director for African American Family Services in Minneapolis, a community organizer, a marketing strategist, and a Certified Military Family Life Consultant and Clinical Director of DV Treatment.

So what is an emerging justice leader?

In this age, where crass individualism, hyper alpha male masculinity and rabid self-interest are "in style and exalted," the role of a justice leader has become even more important. An emerging justice leader is a person of courage who pushes for change regardless of their position, job, or vocation. An emerging justice leader guides and directs organizations, institutions, and people toward action. Action that is founded on the qualities of justness, equitability, service to others, and tapping communal resilience. This person shows great promise and leadership, but also needs support, structure, and accountability. It is not their rhetoric nor their feelings that make them a justice leader; it is their actions and attitude A justice leader is keenly aware of communal and civil restlessness because of systemic and/or implied structural bias. During times of anxiety and strife justice leaders understand the historical intergenerational and personal grieving and mourning of themselves and their community. Justice leaders understand that few things are more undermining to justice work than a justice leader that isn't doing their personal work and practicing self-care and communal deference. Justice leaders have a keen awareness of the inherent tensions between justice and liberty. Justice without an understanding of individual freedoms can lead to stagnation, but liberty without justice can lead to crass individualism and abuse of power. The role of a justice leader is to look for balance in these sometimes competing concepts.

Are You Ready for This Book?

This book is for the emerging justice leaders that need and want more affirmation, more self-care, more softness, and more self-love. In this book, self-care is defined by restoration and reclamation, which are hallmarks for balanced justice endeavors. Justice leaders have a long history in activism with much of it being practice in the context of community.

This book is my beginning offering to you on your journey of self-mastery and a fuller life through the struggle and strife. I hope that you enjoy this book with the spirit of love that it was intended.

Are you an emerging justice leader who wants to start a business or non-profit—or take your current organization to the next level—all while building a more balanced life, and creating a communal legacy you can be proud?

You have a dream. This book will help you birth it and live it.

The tips in this book will focus on your life, your leadership, and your legacy. They will help you:

- Nurture a **life** in which success and self-care complement one another

- Mindfully build and **lead** justice organizations that represent the best of who you are

- Create a **legacy** of love, community, service, and prosperity

This book will help you find your answers. This reading will allow you to discover your unique vision and intelligence. You will learn to nurture the best of what you already have inside you. your innate knowing, wisdom, beauty, and understanding—and your divine energy of service to others, hustling, and hard work.

You will also discover tools, inspiration, and inner strength to rise out of the structures of struggle and strife that hold you back. Whether it's limited opportunities for coaching, mentorship, a lack of access to traditional justice leadership opportunities, or the suffocating role of the strong, hard-driving justice leader who can never ask for help, this book will help you discover that *"self-care and self-love are not weak concept but are important developmental revolutionary acts."* (Micha Grimm, activist)

As an emerging justice leader, the world needs the unique gifts you have to offer. You and your other like-minded brothers and sisters have a long, storied history of strength, resilience, and courage. It is the hope that this book will help you build a life, an organization, and a legacy on this foundation.

We live in a time of pressure and opportunities for emerging justice leaders:

➤ Burnout: Regardless of specific jobs justice leaders have a high rate of burnout, in some cases as much as 30%.

➤ A recent study completed by the state of North Carolina revealed that police agencies across the state experienced an average turnover of 14% in patrol positions. The average tenure for a new officer is 33 months. (North Carolina Criminal Justice Analysis Center, Recruitment and Retention Study Series Sworn Police Personnel, by Douglas L. Yearwood, April 2003.)

➤ Many justice leaders experience extreme isolation, cynicism, and disillusionment towards systems change.

➤ Many justice leaders are being asked to do more and more with less resources and support.

➤ Survival Mode Mentality permeates justice leadership work. Justice leadership provides numerous opportunities to make a positive difference in the lives of others. The survival mentality needs to be socialized out of our leaders, or the status quo will reign supreme.

➤ 57% of pastors would leave the pastorate if they had somewhere else to go or some other vocation they could do.

➤ 70% of pastors don't have any close friends.

➤ 45% of pastors say that they've experienced depression or burnout to the extent that they needed to take a leave of absence from ministry. (Pastorburnout.com)

➤ Research also tells us that 50% to 60% of social justice activists eventually drop out of their cause. (http://integrative.gmu.edu/people/pgorski)

These statistics may seem alarming, but the difference is that we are beginning to talk about them in ways that are not about defects in people. This new understanding creates an opportunity for growth as justice leaders. We are acknowledging that something "happens" to people when they experience difficulties.

Why do I focus this book—and my work as a justice leadership coach—strictly on emerging justice leaders? Here's why: Because, in my other life as a therapist, 15% of my clients have been justice leaders, and one-third of those have been African American. Every day I see what emerging justice leaders are capable of, what holds them back, and how they can get in their own way.

Because, throughout our history, the voices of justice leaders are often ignored, thwarted, or marginalized—through racism, gender bias, or other cultural barriers. In my work as a justice leadership coach, as well as in my job as a therapist, I help emerging justice leaders reclaim their voices and reconnect with the fire that still burns deep inside of them.

Because I'm the grandson of a justice leader; the son of a justice leader; the husband of an amazing, talented African American woman; and the father of an equally amazing and talented African American woman and son that I hope to inspire in them a sense of justice.

I'm the child of a people who have been organizing and fighting for justice for many generations. We were cut out of mainstream economic life for so long that we had to create our own economic survival and success. We succeeded in these efforts largely because of the hard work and communal resilience and spirit.

In the hearts of emerging justice leaders, there beats a service spirit, an inner knowing, and a divine energy of hustling and hard work. In my job as a coach, I help my clients rediscover, reclaim, and tap into all of these.

Why should you pay attention to what I have to say? Because I'm not just a justice leadership coach: I'm also a justice leader myself, and I support justice leaders. I believe that anything that needs to change only happens with a spark, a fire that ignites others. I believe that justice is that community spark that we need to nurture and support as a society.

How to Use This Book

This book and the accompanying online resources and tools are designed to be useful. The book should be read in parts and discussed immediately with others to deepen your understanding. The Life portion of the book sets the stage and foundation for the Leadership part. If you are not a balanced-right person in life, then you will not be an effective mindful leader. The Leadership portion sets the stage for creating a lasting Legacy that can be built. Thoughtful leadership will allow for you to develop a mission/vision which will, in turn, allow your legacy to flourish. This book is not about giving you better tools and words to win the "Oppression Olympics" contest. Many justice leaders look like they are doing service work and talk a good game but can inadvertently recreate shadow copies of the same systems that oppress others. This book is to be used to challenge you to be a better justice leader and person.

This book is designed for self-study and exploration. As stated earlier, there are three primary sections in the book. These sections are **Life**, **Leadership**, and **Legacy** tips. Each chapter is specifically designed to push you toward your most courageous self. At the end of each chapter are self-study questions and insight notes that you can return to in order to further and deepen your study of self.

Life

Winning is great, sure, but if you are going to do something in life, the secret is learning how to lose. Nobody goes undefeated all the time. If you can pick up after a crushing defeat, and go on to win again, you are going to be a champion someday.
– Wilma Rudolph

1) Self-care matters. Make sure that you matter to you.

Self-care has impacts on your health directly. Self-care can aid you in experiencing sensations that refresh, focus and energize you. When you develop self-nurturing routines your body naturally responds with an increase in rational thought processes, memory and determination are more focused, and our relationships are better off for it. Develop self-care plans that incorporate pre-event, during event, and post-recovery strategies after high-activation endeavors.

I am a feminist, and what that means to me is much the same as the meaning of the fact that I am Black: it means that I must undertake to love myself and to respect myself as though my very life depends on upon self-love and self-respect.
– June Jordan

2) Develop a yearly wellness plan.

Develop a holistic annual wellness checkup plan. Schedule doctors' appointments like the OB, mammogram, or prostate checkup, and refill your prescriptions and go pick them up. Although it sounds routine, these are the things that get pushed off our calendars so quickly. Do a new plan at the beginning of each year. Here are the top health concerns for justice leaders to make sure you ask about and address: diabetes, depression, anxiety, asthma, sarcoidosis, lung cancer, breast cancer, high blood pressure.

If you don't like something, change it.
If you can't change it, change your attitude.
– Maya Angelou

3) Cultivate meaningful relationships.

Spending eighty-hours plus with your cell phone and computer each week doesn't count as relationship building. Social interactions with live human beings can add fulfillment and interest, fend off anxiety, and even help with healthily living longer. Real human connections tend to make us happier overall. Happiness can help us be more productive. That date night and time with friends are good for connecting and good for the business of life.

No matter what accomplishments you make,
somebody helped you.
– Althea Gibson

4) Practice mindfulness.

Take time with a higher knowing, time with self, and time to be still and process. Take a break every twenty-five minutes: stand up, take seven breaths, and walk. Going at a fast pace is sometimes considered to be a mark of success. Speed can take its toll on you and your relationships. Taking time to quiet the internal rumblings can feel unproductive, but this time should be cherished and protected.

> *Breathe. Let go. Remind yourself that this very moment is the only one you know you have for sure.*
> – Oprah Winfrey

5) Spend time with a healing professional.

A good, competent healing professional provides a safe place to be you; to be honest about everything that's going on in your life. A healer helps you be gentle and softer with yourself. A healer helps you get to know your better self. When you need to choose a healer, interview as many as possible because when it comes to healers, "FIT" is necessary.

> *When people told me I'd never make it, I listened to the one person who said I could: me.*
> – Shannon Sharpe

6) Let go of toxic relationships.

Toxicity can show itself in different ways, but regardless of the differences, toxic people must be removed. Sometimes these people are family members, friends, and people we love. Many emerging justice leaders have limited time and resources. Toxic people in your life can manipulate that time and those resources. You must think about the relationships in your life. How do they make you feel? How do you react to those people? Are you avoiding interacting with certain individuals and activities? These may be indicators that you're involved in a toxic relationship. Sometimes a good friend or healer can help you navigate through toxic relationships. ***Racism, sexism, bias and white body supremacy can also take a deadly toxic toll on you.***

I am a woman who came from the cotton fields of the
South. From there I was promoted to the washtub. From
there I was promoted to the cook kitchen. And from there
I promoted myself into the business of manufacturing
hair goods and preparations... I have built
my own factory on my own ground.
– Madam C.J. Walker

7) Do fun stuff.

What do you love to do that charges your batteries? What is fulfilling to you? If you had all the money you needed, what would you do with your time? The life of a justice leader can be challenging and grinding; be sure add some fun things.

When it gets harder to love, love harder.
– Van Jones

8) Go book yourself.

You are an excellent, unique novel. Journaling allows the novel to be written and unfold. Take notes during meditation, or write down inspirational quotes from friends. Write out stream of consciousness thoughts and then go back and study them. Journaling is about learning and relearning the self. Journaling forces you to slow down and process feelings and experiences. Journaling helps you transform the rawness of your unconscious mind.

You're not obligated to win. You're obligated to keep
trying to do the best you can every day.
– Marian Wright Edelman

9) Contemplating vs. complaining.

Contemplating is the art of looking at or viewing with continued attention; observe or study thoughtfully. Some justice leaders get this confused with complaining. When you spend time complaining about the obstacles you are facing, you are wasting so much time being negative that you are losing chances to move forward. Instead of thinking of challenges as problems, think of them as opportunities. You might believe there is no correlation between complaining and relational success when, in fact, there is a connection. Life gets better when you know the difference.

You don't make progress by standing on the sidelines,
whimpering and complaining. You make progress
by implementing ideas.
– Shirley Chisholm

10) Being happy is about attitude, not aptitude.

Balancing a justice mission-driven spirit with demands of family and life requires the right approach. An active but settled mind and body, happy upbeat attitude will help you succeed. It has been proven that a person living in a happy state gets much further in just about everything they do. Just as a bad attitude can bring you down, the right attitude and a happy, healthy mind will help you meet your objectives.

The greatest understanding of all time is that a person
can change his future by merely changing his attitude.
– Oprah Winfrey

11) Always be thankful and be thanking always.

Spend time doing an inventory of individuals and things for which you are grateful. You need to be thankful for not only your accomplishments but also your failures/opportunities. Having a grateful attitude is important. A grateful attitude can help you stay humble when you do achieve success. Always say thank you to people, no matter how small the gesture. Thankfulness allows people to feel you and paves the way for trust to develop. Before you spring out of bed in the morning pause and ask yourself this question: "What things am I grateful for in my life no matter how small." You'll be surprised at your answers.

One of the most beautiful things in the world I've ever seen or heard is people laughing, even when there seems to be so little reason for them to laugh.

– D. L. Hughley

12) Make sure you reward those who matter (including yourself).

People in your life need to feel regarded. As a justice leader, you can put your head down and just grind away. That grinding can strain relationships. We can easily stop sending positive vibes to those we love and begin to send negative and or neutral vibes. It's important to take the time to reward people with your time and focused attention. When children do great things, parents will pay them with something nice, whether a kind word of encouragement or something new. When individuals do well in their job, they may get pay increases. As you surpass your justice leadership milestones, reward yourself. Treat yourself to something nice and award yourself or others for a job well done.

*Once we recognize what it is we are feeling, once we
recognize we can feel deeply, love deeply, can feel joy,
then we will demand that all parts of our lives
produce that kind of joy.*

– Audre Lorde

13) Keep your eyes on the prize.

As you become more successful, you may be challenged with bigger obstacles as well as smaller obstacles in your life. Pick your battles wisely and remember balance is the key. While you do need to focus some energy on solving small or minor issues, do not dwell on them and lose precious time and effort when you should be focusing on the bigger picture. That big picture must include meaningful relationships. In other words, do not allow the smaller things to clutter your mind, body and monopolize your time. Keep your eyes on the big picture.

*It's in the act of having to do things that you
don't want to that you learn something about
moving past the self. Past the ego.*

– bell hooks

14) Stress and healing routines.

Being successful means taking care of you and developing healing routines that manage stress, both physically and emotionally. You will need to have energy, focus, as well as rest and settling. In turn, this will help you concentrate and put in the hours required to be successful. Without taking proper care of yourself and managing stress, you will end up struggling, and your service work could feel the effects. Daily healing routine areas should include: mindfulness, moving your body, sleep hygiene, and development of healthy eating habits. Developing a self-care plan that includes pre-care, in-event care, and post-care recovery is important. Include a communication with friends and family outside of your justice work. These last two points are especially true during times of civil restlessness. If you have a Smartphone, download the Daylio app and track your stress days.

It's time for you to move, realizing that the thing you are
seeking is also seeking you.
– Iyanla Vanzant

15) Don't bite.

When developing a support network of people that care for you in explicit and implicit ways, be sure to nurture that network. Refrain from rumor spreading, shunning, and backstabbing. Both men and women can use indirect and micro-aggression in relationships; in a support system, these strategies undermine respect and trustworthiness. Don't bite the network that feeds you.

If you're treated a certain way, you become a particular
kind of person. If certain things are described to you as
being real, they're real for you whether they're real or not.
– James Baldwin

16) Cultivate a support network.

Family ties, friendships and commitment to social activities can offer emerging justice leaders an emotional shield against stress. A strong support system can also help you cope better with relational, business, and community problems. Cultivating support networks can take some effort. The effort is rewarding in the long run because it thwarts the tendency towards isolation. A healthy and diverse social support network can act as a buffer against depression, anxiety, and illness.

It's not the load that breaks you down;
it's the way you carry it.
– Lena Horne

17) Grow a pair.

A connection is essential to a couples' success. Most couples planning for or contemplating marriage start off connected. One of the mistakes that couples make is to take their connection for granted. When trying to be a justice leader connection is especially important. This is partly due to your focus elsewhere. It is important to celebrate your relationship. Develop rituals to mark anniversaries and other relationship moments. These things matter and they aid in the growth of your relationship.

Love is or it ain't. Thin love ain't love at all.
– Toni Morrison

18) Be soft. Be gentle.

Starting a justice endeavor is taxing and is hard, but I don't have to tell you that. The hardness takes many forms: rushing, moving, lack of sleep, making mistakes, and dealing with difficult people. During this time you can be very hard and critical on yourself. It is of vital importance that you find time to bring some softness into your life deliberately. Examples include massages, pedicures, manicures, listening to softer music, experiencing nature, reassuring touches, taking naps, humming, breathing, singing, rocking, using essential oils, affirmations, meditation and guided imagery. These things may bring more balance to your life and help you settle more into softness. If you have a Smartphone, download the Calm app.

If you don't understand yourself,
you don't know anybody else.
– Nikki Giovanni

19)   Out of the mouths of babes.

Children can make us look at things that we never knew were there. Many justice leaders are trying to not only provide for themselves but to secure a future for their children. With that focus, you can sometimes forget what matters to them and what they can teach you. It matters to children that they feel safe and regarded. It matters to them that you confront your selfishness. It matters to them that you develop patience. It matters to them that you are evaluating and reevaluating your priorities. And it also matters that you say "I Love You," regardless of their age.

> *We should all have the opportunity to at least get*
> *a basic education and feel that you*
> *are worthy of something in life.*
> – Jesse Williams

20)   Eat it up.

Justice Leaders often don't waste a second of their day. Your body needs the energy to keep moving. You often work without even breaking for a snack; you may have difficulty concentrating and getting results from the work you're putting in. Eating tweaks can make a big difference in your energy levels, as well as your overall health. Here are a few tweaks: eat breakfast, eat with family, drink more water, prep meals, choose healthy to-go snacks, limit alcohol and drug use, and eat smaller meals more often.

> *I think there are things for all of us to do as long as*
> *we're here and we're healthy.*
> – Gwendolyn Brooks

21) Sleepy head.

Not getting enough sleep can hurt concentration, disturb emotional stability, and increase irritability. An important sleeping tool is to maintain a regular wake and sleeping pattern throughout the week, especially during times of civil restlessness and high activation. High activation can re-trigger secondary, historical, personal and intergenerational trauma responses in your body, which can disrupt sleep. Spending an appropriate amount of time in bed is important. Avoid doing work and watching television in bed. Develop sleep rituals that tell your body that it is time to prep for bed. Avoid stimulants like caffeine, energy drinks and sugar before bed. Regular exercise can promote a restful sleep. A regular bedtime can help set your body's openness to rest and sleep. Keep your sleeping area peaceful and calm. Emerging justice leaders can quickly go into a sleep deficit. Make sure you keep an eye on your sleep.

> *And that call remains true today that we fight for a living, breathing justice — a justice that would have Alton [Sterling] here, and Philando [Castile], and Rekia [Boyd], and Aiyana [Jones], Jamar Clark, and so many people.*
>
> – Deray Mckesson

22) Have a mission-vision.

In justice work having a mission-vision and pursuing it is an important ethic. From John Brown and his mission-vision of freedom for people other than himself to Jane Elliot and her mission-vision to create a more equitable world. To succeed, you need to have dreams and aspirations. Be honest and loving with yourself as to what you want out of life and what you want to give of your life. Allow yourself to dream and think big. Believe that your expression of the mission-vision is what the world needs right this moment.

Never be afraid to sit awhile and think.
– Lorraine Hansberry

23) Never give in, never give up.

When striving to be a successful justice leader, you will meet roadblocks. Remember to keep your head up. There is always a pull to give in or give up: Don't. You can take a break to reimagine and reorganize. This world needs your unique strength and beauty. To reach success, you have to persevere. Even MLK had to learn this. When he was along with his community trying to create a more just world, it took him many times to get it right. Keep striving, even when it becomes challenging.

Injustice anywhere is a threat to justice everywhere.
– Martin Luther King, Jr.

24) Look at the woman in the mirror.

The best way to be great at anything and to be successful is to face the parts of ourselves that are weaker than other parts. Everyone has these parts that need to be strengthened. This process is called "looking at yourself in the mirror" When you find one of your limitations, confront it. Inside of every limitation is a virtue waiting to be discovered. You have to develop the fortitude to sit with it and not run from it. Look at the woman/man in the mirror and see how beautiful they can become.

You never find yourself until you face the truth.
– Pearl Bailey

25) Strong justice leader trap.

Being a justice leader can be isolating in many ways: Less access to resources, business support structures, minimal connections, and navigating the history of racism and white body supremacy. Another isolating concept is the Strong Justice Leader trap. It's a stereotype. It's this corner that this society has regulated you to. It is a trap. Here is the nutshell of it. You nurture everyone around you, and you advocate for others whether they want you to or not. You stoically override the physical and mental pain, and you come through, intact on the other side without self-advocacy. You keep hush about the suffering out of guilt and unbalanced obligation to an unrealistic ideal. The key is to recognize the trap and ask for support. You are not defective. You are not weak. You are not a failure. And self-advocacy is not betrayal: It is one of the most nurturing things you can do. So cry a little sometimes; you deserve it.

*My private past and pain have been used as jokes
and fodder to discredit me and the greater movement
for justice in America.*

– Shaun King

26) Breaking bad.

As a justice leader, you can get into neutral or negative life ruts and habits that do not help you progress, but that you get used to having around. Negative lifestyle habits, regardless of size or nature, can be exceptionally difficult to break. These life patterns can show up in relationships, in business, and in self-care strategies. These habits can be broken, but only if they are examined. Do you procrastinate? Do you put yourself last always? Do you have a short fuse? Breaking these types of habits will take a lot of effort, but you can do it. Poor habits can be the one aspect of your behavior that could be the obstacle to your success. This area of accountability coaching is my specialty. You have to make the changes to enjoy life and be as successful as you desire. Breaking bad habits is one of the keys to success. If you need help, my contact information for coaching is in the back of this book.

> *Don't feel entitled to anything you didn't*
> *sweat and struggle for.*
> – Marian Wright Edelman

27) Being nice attracts.

Being nice in life isn't a strategy or act to get what you want. People you interact with can experience you as authentic or not. People operate off of "vibes" they get from others. Vibes are communal languages. Good vibes attract people to you, and negative or neutral vibes can repel. Cultivate niceness by observing your non-verbal cues as well as your attitude toward people and things. You can also ask people that you trust what they think. Study after study has shown that people with a pleasing sense about themselves have an easier time reaching success. Not only are they more levelheaded in handling the ups and downs of justice work but they also draw people around them who are willing to help with their mission-vision. Being pleasing, being polite, showing genuine interest, and having a great sense of humor costs you nothing and can have significant payoffs.

> *Sometimes, I feel discriminated against, but it does not*
> *make me angry. It merely astonishes me.*
> *How can any deny themselves the pleasure of my*
> *company? It's beyond me.*
> – Zora Neale Hurston

28) Seeing is believing.

So you want to be a justice leader. Well, one thing you need to nurture is a strong belief in yourself. When the people see your confidence and your faith in yourself, they are more likely to believe in your mission. Your confidence will get you through the challenges and build credibility with and in your movement.

You know, you do need mentors, but in the end,
you just need to believe in yourself.

– Diana Ross

29) Appreciate life.

Being a successful justice leader isn't an easy road. Intense focus is mandatory. There are times when you are working on your mission-vision and you are working a regular job to keep food on the table. Sometimes when you are focusing you can forget that community and connections outside of your focus matter. Appreciate life, people, work, and everything around you. Learn as much as you can from every person you meet. Do not turn people away when you do not agree with them. You never know the very people you turn away may be the very people that come to your rescue during a time of difficulty or may be the ideal partner or ally. Never burn life, individuals, and bridges – and if you have, repair them.

I have a lot of things to prove to myself.
One is that I can live my life fearlessly.

– Oprah Winfrey

30) Body strong, mind strong.

As you work to achieve your dream, don't forget that your body matters. Strength training for justice leaders is important, especially as you get older. If you do not use your muscles, you will lose your muscles over time. An active body helps you concentrate better, can add confidence to your vibe, and can help manage stress. Start with light weights and use them throughout your range of motion. Always consult your doctor and an exercise professional before starting any exercise regime.

> *Everything that happens to you is a reflection of what you believe about yourself. We cannot outperform our level of self-esteem. We cannot draw to ourselves more than we think we are worth.*
>
> – Iyanla Vanzant

31) Therapy is not a four-letter word, but help is.

Justice leaders have some of the same mental health concerns as others, with greater stressors due to activation, adversarial system responses, racism, prejudice, and economic disparities. Many justice leaders shy away from therapy as a potential solution to depression, anxiety, marriage problems, and parenting issues. Concerns about therapist or treatment process and judgment are real, but if you are having difficulty in your life, marriage, or mental health circumstances, there is no shame in asking for help and support from a professional. Your success as a justice leader can sometimes be helped by addressing some of these concerns.

> *We can say "Peace on Earth." We can sing about it, preach about it, or pray about it, but if we have not internalized the mythology to make it happen inside us, then it will not be.*
>
> – Betty Shabazz

32) Trauma drama.

Some justice communities have had a long, brutal history of trauma. Justice leaders that have a mission of working with policing, spiritual reform, social justice, and poverty and GLBTQ issues know trauma and brutality. During most of that history, treatment was not available for you, but it is now. Personal, historical trauma and intergenerational trauma may have impacts on your coping strategies. Anything that has happened to you individually or to your community as a collective and has happened too fast, too soon, or was too much may be impacting on pervasive and PTSD symptoms. If you think trauma may be affecting you, seek help from a qualified trauma therapist. Part of our work as justice leaders is to create transformed, informed processes and environments for the benefit of our communities, justice partners, and workers. Trauma healing is a good place to start. My contact info is in the back of this book.

There was trauma and never any treatment or acknowledgment of what the trauma did to those that were enslaved or their progeny. Black people are "profoundly resilient," posits DeGruy, but the fact is, they have been traumatized.

– Dr. Joy Degruy

33) Learn a new life skill.

Learning new life skills will enhance your success. Learning new life skills will make you flexible and adaptable. Being flexible is important in life and leadership. What are the things in your life you would like to provide? What type of person does your community appreciate? Talk with people in your life who are good at it and try to implement a strategy. I am an exceptional justice leadership coach in this area and would love the opportunity to coach you. If you want to become an outstanding justice leader, learn all there is about the types of person that you want for the communities you service.

> *The paradox of education is precisely this; that as one begins to become conscious, one begins to examine the society in which he is being educated.*
> – James Baldwin

34) Try Tai Chi.

When working for your dreams as hard as you do, there are times when you have to slow it down. A fantastic exercise to do this is Tai Chi. Tai Chi is a gentle exercise where there is a continuous motion from one position to the next. It aids stress and anxiety reduction, improves flexibility and balance, which can minimize injuries. Tai Chi is low impact and puts minimal stress on muscles and joints, making it safe for people at most age and fitness levels. Consider doing it with others also. Communal movements can help us experience more in-synchness. Always consult your doctor and fitness professional before starting any new program.

> *We must not, in trying to think about how we can make a big difference, ignore the small daily differences we can make, which, over time, add up to big differences that we often cannot foresee.*
> – Marian Wright Edelman

35) Declaration of independence.

Declare your independence from the chains of the past. Declare your independence from others' expectations. Declare your independence from the status quo. Move out and capture the future you. Do not be afraid to go for what you know is the right thing for you. Being independent allows you to take control over your destiny and emotional state. Stand firm in what you believe and do not permit other people to determine how you feel or what you believe in.

> *Someone is always at my elbow reminding me that I am*
> *the granddaughter of enslaved people.*
> *It fails to register depression with me.*
> – Zora Neale Hurston

36) Paint a perfect portrait.

An excellent way to keep working toward your life goals is to see it. If you want to open a loving relationship, a more connected family, or a more peaceful home, find a picture or article about a successful family or relationship or quiet home and study how it got done. Some justice leaders have had success using a vision board. A vision board is a pictorial representation of where you would like to be in the future. It can help you focus and refocus on what's important. Another tool is to visualize yourself reaching your goal throughout your day. This is another way to slow down hectic days. Seeing believes. Paint a beautiful portrait of what you desire in life. You can create a vision board by cutting pictures from magazines and arranging them as you see your life. To bring clarity, it sometimes helps to have two vision boards: one for your justice life and the other for your personal life. Google Vision Boards for ideas.

> *You may encounter many defeats, but you must not be*
> *defeated. In fact, it may be necessary to encounter the*
> *defeats, so you can know who you are, what you can*
> *rise from, how you can still come out of it.*
> – Maya Angelou

37)   Each one teach one.

You have a gift. There is something you know that others do not. You have an interest that others find fascinating. Think about that thing you do that makes you smile or feel good. Now teach one person about that thing. The skills that you develop in the process will help you in your justice leadership journey. Notice the passion and the interest as you teach it. Cultivate it and harness it. It is the fuel for your future.

> *The question is not whether we can afford to invest in*
> *every child; it is whether we can afford not to.*
> – Marian Wright Edelman

38)   Expand your mind and your life will follow.

Okay, take a moment. Get a picture in your mind of what personal and professional success is. Got it? Okay, now what would it look like if you pushed it even further. Whatever your idea of achievement, take it one step further. Stretch your mind and reach just one inch higher than you thought you could reach.

> *I think the range of emotions and perceptions*
> *I have had access to as a black person and as a female*
> *person are greater than those of people who are neither....*
> *So it seems to me that my world did not shrink because*
> *I was a black woman writer. It just got bigger.*
> – Toni Morrison

39) Be taught.

Take some classes where you can get a certification in the expertise of your passion. Enhancing yourself on a personal level will improve everything about you, making you feel better, about the person you are. When you feel better, you achieve more.Right now is a great time to obtain your certification in some other outside interest.

> *I freed a thousand of the enslaved. I could have freed a thousand more if only they knew they were enslaved.*
> – Harriet Tubman

40) Stress can't be avoided but stressing can.

When you strive to be a successful justice leader, stress is a natural part of the process. The key is to do everything you can to avoid stressing. Adding unnecessary stress into the equation will take the focus away from accomplishing your life and justice goals. This can cause distress in your body and many times in your relationships, both communal and personal. When you start feeling overwhelmed, stop, change direction, and avoid stressing. The only thing stressing accomplishes is draining your thinking power and creativity.

> *When there is no enemy within,*
> *the enemies outside cannot hurt you.*
> – African Proverb

SELF-STUDY QUESTIONS AND INSIGHTS

What are the top 10 life tips that stood out to you and why?

1)

2)

3)

4)

5)

6)

7)

8)

9)

10)

What insights did you get from the quotes in this section?

What did this section make you feel?

NEXTWORD

I am a mother and an activist. Most people would assume that most mothers are activists of some sort. However, the kind of activist that I have become requires that I work from the inside out. Meaning that when something touches me personally, I make the connection from my personal reality to the global community. Along the way to my personal solution, I find people that are experiencing a similar problem. Before long I have cultivate a network of people that are not the same but similar in that we all are searching relief.

Being a mother gives me the tenacity. I'm like a dog with a bone when it comes to mychildren. I will not let it go, I will not give up. My connecting to my children requires that I stay the course and have the tough conversations. Mothering a Black boy made me acutely aware of the danger that a Black boy might face. His father and I took on the idea that it was our job to protect his potential. Being a mother facilitates a love for the child that burns in your belly. Its not a love that is romantic or romanticizes. Nothing can quench it. I have found that it is love that leads you, not fear. I lead with love.

The activist/organizer in me relies on strategy. I'm not afraid to confront or combat as a part of strategy. My strategy is anchored in research. The data supports my positions which based on principles of justice, equity and liberation. In other words. I believe that I am right which doesn't mean that I am right. I have learned that being a leader is not about being right. It is about being willing. Willing to go with a group rather than go alone. Willling to be wrong – dead wrong. Willing to build commonwealth.

I never aspired to be a leader. My son's food allergies and the need to feed him propelled me forward into the world of food justice. For that work, I am called a leader in my field. I accept that title, it is a high honor. Yet I do not claim the title for myself. I believe that Iam more like a consultant – a consultant on all things community.

Often, I am asked how to replicate my work on local food access. It's really something that I have avoided. I believe that the answer to community issues are found within the community asking the question. Landscape Architect Jans Jenson said best "every community has the intellect to heal itself."

Realizing that leadership is more about surrender than it is control allows me to see that the potential is within our communities but it must be facilitated or awakened. Like the love I feel for my son I feel love for community. That love isn't as personal as a mother and son. It is the love of the whole of humanity. Love allows me to see beyond the present situation and not be discouraged by racism, exploitation, poverty, etc. Love or agape allows me to see the divinity in all things and realize that what we are unmaking with my justice work is that divinity.

As a mother, it is my job to help my children uncover their potential. Through a deep love and commitment, protecting the potential of my children from all things that could hurt my children. Nothing rival this commitment.

My role as a mother offers me the change to doula the community where I live. Helping community give birth to itself is sacred work and it must be insulated by love. To lead the community means to serve the community. Assisting community residents reimage a world that is vibrant and thriving is an opportunity to serve my children and every future generation.

– LaDonna Azziza Redmond,
Mother, Doula, Activist

Leadership

I think we have to rethink the concept of "leader." 'Cause "leader" implies "follower." And, so many - not so many, but I think we need to appropriate, embrace the idea that we are the leaders we've been looking for.

– Grace Lee Boggs

41)   Have vision for your quest.

One thing that justice leaders have is vision. Vision allows leaders to stay the course when things get rocky. Vision allows others to know what they are following. It fosters clarity. Leaders have an imperative to succeed; you need to have a vision and aspirations. Be honest with yourself as to what you want out of your justice work and what you want to give of your life. Allow your mind to dream big. The energy must force you out of your comfort zone for you become the leader that the world needs.

There are still many causes worth sacrificing for, so much history yet to be made.

– Michelle Obama

42) Make a plan or plan to fail.

You have a great idea that will bring to you what you need and what you desire. But if you don't create a mission-vision plan as your very first step, then you are planning to fail. Whether you will be searching for partners to build structural change or to fund an international justice practice or not, this plan will be the blueprint for your success. The mission-vision plan will consist of social trends, financial strategy planning, problem analysis, exit strategies, communal care planning, civil unrest, communal core planning strategies and community ICS plan, social marketing and promotional options, everything about your goal. When going to communities and partners, you will be required to have a plan. If your success were personal, you would want to create a plan. A mission-vision plan would be a good option to allow you to keep track of everything involving your goal. I am an excellent justice leadership coach when it comes to creating a mission-vision plan. If interested contact me, a free 30 minute consult is available. My information is in the back of this book.

> *We will be ourselves and free, or die in the attempt.*
> *Harriet Tubman was not our*
> *great-grandmother for nothing.*
> – Alice Walker

43) Mindful leadership.

Mindfulness justice leadership is the ability to actively notice the subtle and overt indicators in your team and in the communities you service. Conscious leadership helps you realize that there are no positive or negative outcomes, just current limitations and opportunities. Aware justice leaders ask a lot of questions with a tone of openness and an eye on learning. If you value guidance and receiving direction through fostering balanced cooperation, then you are a mindful justice leader. Mindful justice leadership isn't only about the bottom line and winning and losing. Mindful leadership is about nurturing transparency to those around you. When you model mindfulness and find ways to encourage mindfulness in your justice endeavors, you and your partners build greater individual and community resilience. In turn, your organization and partnerships become more flexible, creative, and resilient too.

> *Never underestimate the power of dreams and the*
> *influence of the human spirit. We are all the same*
> *with this idea: The potential for greatness*
> *lives within each of us.*
>
> – Wilma Rudolph

44) Promote potential in others.

As a mindful justice leader, the greatest responsibility we have is to support others in reaching for what is best for them and promoting it. It is our duty to help others to live as close to their unique potential as we can. With everything we say and do, we're impacting other people we care for. The ideal is to do this with consideration and intention. Believe in them: You may be the only one. Be a model for potential. Challenge and encourage the best in them. Share yourself and be present.

> *Is solace anywhere more comforting than*
> *that in the arms of a sister?*
>
> – Alice Walker

45) Tap into your potential.

To succeed at anything, you need to see that you have the ability to reach your goals. Tapping into your potential means that you do the work and study to find what that potential is.

You must explore interests as well as be exposed to things that don't interest you. Having a diverse repertoire of experience helps you be flexible in decision making and course corrections. Study others to see what they can teach you. Get a mentor and nurture the relationship. A journey always starts with the first step and the first step in potential is knowledge-gathering.

> *Whatever we believe about ourselves and*
> *our ability comes true for us.*
> – Susan L. Taylor

46) Look back but don't stay back.

One thing that you will learn as an emerging justice leader is that everyone has failures or mistakes from the past. To have success, you need to learn from your past and value those difficult lessons, but do not ever dwell on the past. Simply move forward and make improved, better-educated decisions from the experiences. Your mistakes are only bricks in the road towards your inevitable success.

> *I get angry about things, then go on and work.*
> – Toni Morrison

47) Nurture an unstoppable attitude.

As you push yourself to dream forward, your most formidable weapon is your attitude. Bumps and bruises come with the experience of being a justice leader. You need to have determination. There might be associates, friends, or family members who feel it would be better if you focused your attention in another direction. Uphold your unstoppable attitude and be determined to succeed.

*Greatness is not measured by what a man or woman
accomplishes, but by the opposition he or she
has overcome to reach his goals.*

– Dorothy Height

48) Do what you enjoy.

What is the reason that you are working your tail off to make this work? The more clarity you have, the more chances of succeeding. An essential element of success is enjoyment. You should focus your efforts on the things that you enjoy. Reality is when you find that thing that you enjoy; it doesn't feel like work. As you start out, make a list of everything you find interesting about your justice endeavor. When you recognize your talents and skills, then focus yourself in that area.

*Success is liking you, liking what you do,
and liking how you do it.*

– Maya Angelou

49) With an eye toward the past and on toward the future.

Being a justice leader is about noticing the building blocks to create a transformational justice collective infrastructure. Ultimately it means that you partner with others to develop sustained care community for justice workers and those they serve. It means creating care cooperatives that nurture communal ways of incorporating the young, elderhood development and attention, shared self-care language and rituals. As a justice leader, you must look at justice work through the lifespan. How do we care for older justice leaders who have given so much? How do we nurture the justice leaders coming behind us? How do we do this with a planned-out, thoughtful, loving, structure with communal benchmarks, and accountability?

Great leadership isn't shaped in the absence of opposition
but the presence of it. Great leaders draw us together by
our universal humanity; they galvanize the wills of the
willing; they draw clarity from the spigot of chaos.

– Charles M. Blow

50) R.E.S.P.E.C.T.

As a justice leader, you must make sure that all your partners
feel they are a vital to you and the justice endeavors. Expressing
to your partners that you recognize their worth will motivate
them. Try to learn from their expertise and encourage them to
act like experts in their fields.

I'm going to continue to stand with the people
that are being oppressed.

– Colin Kaepernick

51) Go where others won't.

When you aren't afraid to go into the unknown, you find new
worlds and opportunities. The other benefit is that to create
new worlds of your design. There's no right way to do anything.
Go against the grain, go with your gut, be a justice pioneer, and
don't do what others are already doing.

Sometimes you have to raise a little hell
to get some heaven.

– Joe Madison

52) You had me at *hello, not really.*

Justice leaders must have an undying belief in their mission-
vision, but we wouldn't be human if we never had doubts.
The most important thing is to be in love with your mission
of service time and time again. Loving service will probably
change over time, and that's fine.

*I was never quiet when I worked at CNN when we did
dumb stuff. You can't just take the check and stay quiet.
Truth demands a voice: speak up.*

– Roland Martin

53) Don't talk about it be about it.

As an emerging justice leader you work very hard for the people
and organizations you serve. Partners and community members
must believe that your particular justice endeavor will succeed
no matter how tough things get. Being an emerging justice
leader is about hustling for the divine purpose of service to
others and cultivating opportunity and partnerships.

*In your struggle for freedom, justice, and equality I am
with you. I came to Louisville because I could not remain
silent while my people, many I grew up with, many I went
to school with, many my blood relatives, were being
beaten, stomped, and kicked in the streets simply because
they want freedom, and justice and equality in housing.*

– Muhammad Ali

54) Be humble.

It might seem counterintuitive but having humility takes more
wisdom than craving glory. Your partners and community will
appreciate it and develop more trust in you and the vision. A
mindful justice leader understands the difference between
being a leader and a boss. Both are in charge, but a justice leader
shares the limelight and is comfortable giving them the credit
that they richly deserve.

*If the road to social transformation can be paved
only by saints who never make mistakes,
the road will never be built.*

– Van Jones

55) Openly communicate.

A justice leader understands that the benefits of open communication are imperative, both in the service and in life. Outstanding justice leaders place great importance on making sure they are included, and they know the importance of listening. Open two-way communication will have your service endeavor skyrocketing onward and upward, easing through the curves. Commit to regular one-on-one meetings with the principal partners and being briefed on the leading projects to ensure you know where things stand throughout a service endeavor. I am excellent at coaching justice leaders in developing dashboard communication reporting structures and two-way communication tools that provide pertinent information flow to frontline and partnership levels of a service endeavor.

> *And let's just be honest, there is no such place called "justice," if by justice we envision a finish line, or a point at which the battle is won and the need to continue the struggle over. After all, even when you succeed in obtaining a measure of justice, you're always forced to mobilize to defend that which you've won. There is no looming vacation. But there is redemption in the struggle.*
> – Tim Wise

I give free 30 minute consults. My information is in the back of this book.

56) Meeting needs.

Time is money. So time spent in meetings must be productive and, above all else, useful. You should want to limit time wasters like lecturing during meetings. Trust your team to do their assignments. Avoid micromanaging, and utilize clear agenda and meeting management tools.

I will not have my life narrowed down.
I will not bow down to somebody else's whim
or to someone else's ignorance.

– bell hooks

57) Great leaders let other lead.

Great justice leaders nurture others to lead. Leadership can be found at all levels in justice organizations. Identify influence leaders in your service endeavors and help them to develop their leadership skills. Transferring of organizational knowledge through mentoring allows you to build strong leadership skills and channels in your service to others.

Surround yourself with only people who are
going to lift you higher.

– Oprah Winfrey

58) Mind on your money and your money on your mind.

As a justice leader, your financial literacy is vital to the future of your service to others. Knowing your numbers will not only be crucial for your service endeavor to grow. You do need to be up-to-date from the beginning on what it costs to produce successful justice outcomes for those you service. If this is not one of your strengths, educate yourself and get a mentor and ask them to teach you.

One thing that's true is that whether you are making
a financial investment or an investment of the heart,
you usually get what you give. What's also true is that
investing the wrong assets into the wrong places is a great
way to end up broke (or broken).

– Dr. Boyce Watkins

59) Confidence and optimism are attractive.
There are challenges that a justice endeavor goes through during
the operation. In these trying times, a justice leader must exude
confidence and optimism to encourage partners to believe in
the justice effort and service.

> *I used to want the words "She tried" on my tombstone.*
> *Now I want "She did it."*
> — Katherine Dunham

60) Promote a learning environment.
A justice leader recognizes that increased knowledge, more
experience, and challenging different mindsets increase
community satisfaction, motivation, and productivity.
Frequently encourage all levels of the service endeavor to think
creatively and promote alternate perspectives.

> *If you don't understand yourself,*
> *you don't understand anybody else.*
> — Nikki Giovanni

61) Common togetherness.
A team has individuals with diverse strengths and
understandings, often conflicting. A justice leader makes sure
that the focus remains on the process of completing common
goals. It is vital to challenge myopic personal points of view to
create organizational goals that foster togetherness.

> *The humanity part for me is the first step. And that's what*
> *it's always been. It hasn't been about the anthem.*
> — David West

62) Manage conflict.

In most human interactions conflict is inevitable. As a justice leader, it is mandatory that you create a wellness-oriented environment that resolves internal conflicts within the team at the very beginning of the service endeavor. A clear thought-out process for resolving a conflict that everyone is familiar with at every level is critical to the success of your service effort. Even fundamental issues, when dealt with maturity, can be resolved quickly without leaving long-term organizational damage. Differences should not hinder your team's performance. As partners go through conflict together and build a common language and understanding, trust is cultivated and sustained.

To sit back and do nothing is to cooperate
with the oppressor.

– Jane Elliott

63) Great leaders delegate.

Great justice leaders don't try to do it all themselves. Great justice leaders realize very quickly that they must divide the work and delegate, then support and create a reporting system that checks the results. Delegation demonstrates trust in the team and fosters individual and cultural growth within the service endeavor.

No matter what accomplishments you make,
somebody helped you.

– Althea Gibson

64) Get a life.

As a justice leader, you need to find practical ways to cultivate a culture of self-care and balance for your partners. Justice leaders pay attention to the stress levels of their partners and constantly try and effect change in the environment to mediate. Modeling and encouraging partners to explore and share self-care strategies can go a long way to have healthy justice service endeavors. Whether it's promoting listening to music on the commute home, turning off the cell phone and email during personal or family time, or participating in a social activity or hobby, keeps your commitment to making sure that your partners have a life outside of work.

> *The kind of beauty I want most is the hard-to-get kind that comes from within – strength, courage, dignity.*
> – Ruby Dee

65) Get up and get out.

Make sure that you encourage your partners to take stress breaks. Have them get up and walk around, get outside for some fresh air. Encourage your partners to develop self-care plans that incorporate pre-event, during the event, and post-recovery strategies after high activation endeavors. Promote some deep breathing, light stretching, or just close your eyes for one minute. Taking a mental or physical break is an important strategy and helps your partners deal with day-to-day stress and create a better work environment, which improves your service to others, bottom line.

> *You are on the eve of a complete victory. You can't go wrong. The world is behind you.*
> – Josephine Baker

66) You got to move it move it.

Developing a regular exercise wellness program for your justice organization is one of the best ways to limit the negative health issues that come with the demands of building a service endeavor. Under stress we build up certain hormones; exercise dissipates some of them. Make a commitment to encouraging exercising at least 30 minutes, four times a week. Also, incorporate healthy practices such as a walking group, eating more fruits and vegetables while reducing added sugars, fat, and sodium. Encourage community strategies for wellness. Also encourage your employees and community partners to get regular physical health and wellness checkup. Always consult your doctor when starting an exercise regime.

> *There is nothing better than adversity.*
> *Every defeat, every heartbreak, every loss, contains*
> *its own seed, its own lesson on how to improve*
> *your performance the next time.*
> −Malcolm X

67) Toxic avenger.
Toxic people can poison your environment and undermine your mission-vision. As a leader, if you are serious about reaching your goal and being successful, you will need to rid your life of these toxic people as soon as they reveal themselves. While you may not be able to get them out of your partnership immediately, you should minimize the amount of damage that they can do to you and your reputation.

> *Being a victim of oppression in the United States is not*
> *enough to make you revolutionary, just as dropping out of*
> *your mother's womb is not sufficient to make you human.*
> *People who are full of hate and anger against their*
> *oppressors or who only see Us versus Them can make a*
> *rebellion but not a revolution. The oppressed internalize*
> *the values of the oppressor. Therefore, any group that*

*achieves power, no matter how oppressed, is not going to
act differently from their oppressors as long as they have
not confronted the values that they have internalized
and consciously adopted different values.*

– Grace Lee Boggs

68) Fear and failure.

Fear of failure is a normal emotion for every person on the planet. As a leader, there will be times where you have to help your partners get past that fear because it is the determining factor between failing and succeeding. You can do that by setting realistic goals and then examining those goals with your partners, and on occasion do any necessary realignment. Above all, believe in imparting to your partners that you believe in them.

*When I dare to be powerful – to use my strength in
the service of my vision, then it becomes less and less
important whether I am afraid.*

–Audre Lorde

69) Promoting a winning attitude.

Mindful justice leaders must have the right attitude for success. Creating a positive working environment and surrounding yourself with partners that share a positive attitude will help you succeed. Do not allow negative mind states slip into your service endeavor. Promote attendance to motivational seminars and find ways to help your partners enjoy life. A good attitude will enable you to turn any bad situation into learning opportunities. The results of a winning attitude are that the culture of your partners will feel better; your partners will have more energy and have a much higher opportunity for success. Create healing spaces and mixers for partners to commune.

Never underestimate the power of dreams and the influence of the human spirit. We are all the same in this notion: The potential for greatness lives within each of us.
                                                        –Wilma Rudolph

70)   Sweat the small things.

When things are small and do not appear to have a significant impact on the big picture, justice leaders need to ensure that partners focus and follow through in completing their tasks. Not paying attention to those little things can quickly add up to a big mess and become very costly in both resources and reputation.

This goes back 400 years; we're not going to solve this in one or two years. But we have to acknowledge that this exists. Stop sweeping [racism] under the rug.
                                                        – Shannon Sharpe

71)   A heaping helping of praise.

Be mindful of always offering praise. Your partners are an important part of your success and by providing recognition and support, they will, in return, show dedication and work hard to help your service endeavor reach its mission-vision goal. Give praise in the company of others and critique with the individual in private. Praise can be reinforced myriad ways. Research has been proven that people will work harder for an award or a title than they will for an increase in pay.

Give light, and people will find the way.
                                                        – Ella Baker

72) Encourage collaboration.

As a justice leader, you will reach various times when you and some of your partners do not have the appropriate expertise to accomplish outstanding mission-vision goals. This is the time to encourage collaboration and networking among partners that would normally not interact with each other. These relationships can help you and your team answer questions, be provided guidance, and receive the ongoing support and encouragement you will need.

> *I always wanted to be somebody. If I made it, it's half because I was game enough to take a lot of punishment along the way and half because there were a lot of people who cared enough to help me.*
> —Althea Gibson

73) The both/and leader.

Justice leaders of today need to be tech savvy and people-focused. On the surface, you may think that these skills are juxtaposed to each other. Tech savvy justice leaders have tendencies that lean analytical, structured, and process. People-focused justice leaders have tendencies that lean empathetic, social, and engaging. Justice leaders assess their skills and see where they can improve and get mentoring or support in both of these areas. Today's multi-generational justice leaders need to be more flexible than before.

> *Success doesn't come to you...you go to it.*
> —Marva Collins

74) Nurture communal relationships

Keep your line of communication open with your service community. If they have a problem, show them they deserve respect and resolve the issue quickly. Make occasional phone calls to see if they have any needs. This will let your service community know that you are there for them and care about their success. This relationship is what is going to keep you on the road to becoming that exceptional justice leader.

> *Nobody's free until everybody's free.*
> –Fannie Lou Hamer

75) Reflections in the mirror may be closer than they appear.

Reflect on what you have accomplished; evaluate your service to others milestones to ensure you are still heading in the right direction. Remember as a justice leader repositioning yourself, your service endeavor and your partners along the way to success are entirely reasonable and to be expected. Rather than continue to battle an issue, reflect on what has not been working, and reposition so you do not have to keep repeatedly fighting the same things. This doesn't mean giving up the essentials of your mission-vision.

> *Weakness is what brings ignorance, cheapness, racism,*
> *homophobia, desperation, cruelty, brutality, all these*
> *things that will keep a society chained to the ground;*
> *one foot nailed to the floor.*
> – Henry Rollins

SELF-STUDY QUESTIONS AND INSIGHTS

What are the top 10 leadership tips that stood out to you and why?

1)

2)

3)

4)

5)

6)

7)

8)

9)

10)

What insights did you get from the quotes in this section?

What did you experience as you read this section?

What are your next 3 steps to apply what you have learned?

1)

2)

3)

AFTERWORD

The body seeks to survive. Each one of our bodies seeks to survive. This instinct for survival is older and faster than any of our belief systems about how the world should be. Our instinct for survival has no problem with contradicting our deepest held values, if it means that at the end of the day, we will be ok.

This is true for everyone and yet, there's a particular intensity about this when thinking about racial justice and, in particular, when thinking about white people and racial justice. For most multi-generational white U.S.-ers, this need for survival is deeply tied to their whiteness. Systems of racism and white body supremacy in this country have literally hijacked the body's survival responses so that they work in service to keeping those systems in place. And white people, often unintentionally, respond out of this survival system rather than out of their true desire for justice and equity. Whiteness has a life of its own. It can shift and change its shape and form, like a virus, until it has reprogrammed how a body understands what is happening in any given situation, all so that it can ensure its own survival. White resistance, white fragility, microaggressions; these are all examples of survival responses that are fighting, fleeing and freezing in response to racialized moments. White people leaving or avoiding conversations about race, feeling despair or resignation before the work even starts, or refusing to acknowledge that racism is happening, even as people of color are sharing their personal experiences and emotional responses.

Each time these things happen, the white body's survival responses are triggered which means that the body is acting as though its life truly is threatened and has to respond to guarantee its own safety. And safety, in these situations, usually means, for the body, doing anything necessary to come back to a calm and safe state. Generally, this means anything but responding directly to what is happening or pushing for any kind of change.

Dealing with this is not covered in most equity trainings because this is not about what a person learns but instead, about what kind of person you are. This is about a leadership that is able to be in the present moment with whatever is taking place and to respond, not out of triggered reaction, but by assessing every situation through the lens of justice.

The 101 tips in this book are tips that support all kinds of leaders to be awake and able to struggle with what is really happening in front of them rather than with the learned bias and historical reactions that they have been raised with. For white leaders who care deeply about justice, to not do the kind of work outlined in this book is to live in contradiction. The survival responses are triggered long before the mind begins building reason and understanding. This is how whiteness gets recentered in moments when, seemingly, white leaders are trying to confront it. This is personal. It is held in the body. It has to be confronted in the body. Practices like those outlined in this book are part of the work of confronting them.

Do this work alone. Do it with other white people. And while doing this work on yourself, don't stop working to shift the systems at the same time. Full liberation depends on both.

– Susan Raffo,
Bodyworker, Writer,
Community Organizer,
The People's Movement Center,
Minneapolis, MN

Legacy

*Courage is the most important of all the virtues because
without courage you can't practice any other virtue
consistently. You can practice any virtue erratically, but
nothing consistently without courage.*

– Maya Angelou

76) Dream the dream.

What does it mean to succeed? Is it having money, cars, big
houses, material comforts, and accolades? Or is it that you
have created something that transcends time and space?
Is something that is left after you depart that helps the next
communal constructs live and breathe? Is it a knowledge of self
that allows people to be free? As an emerging justice leader, your
answers to those questions will help you determine if what you
are building is a demonstration or a legacy. No judgment either
way. You need to have dreams and aspirations. Be honest with
yourself as to what you want out of life and what you want
to give of your life. Allow your mind to dream and think big.
Thinking bigger than you is how legacies are built.

*You don't make progress by standing on the sidelines,
whimpering and complaining. You make progress
by implementing ideas.*

– Shirley Chisholm

77) Community room.

Regardless of what your goal for success is, get involved with your community. First, get involved with town meetings, understand the local politics, relationships, history, structure, and attend community functions. Legacy is rarely built in isolation. It is constructed in constant interaction with others and community. Questions about what matters and who needs what are surfaced and answered in community. Purpose develops as you listen and ask questions. You will be amazed at the amount of room for use available right there in your neighborhood.

> *Blackness is a state of mind, and I identify with the black community. Mainly, because I realized, early on, when I walk into a room, people see a black woman, they don't see a white woman. So out of that reason alone, I identify more with the black community.*
>
> – Halle Berry

78) Don't pass on debt.

Building your legacy means that you take time to get any debts paid off, especially credit card debts that will cost you a fortune in interest and hinder the flexibility of the next leaders that you have groomed. This is especially important if you will be seeking future partners as a part of your legacy success. You want to ensure that your records and credit are clean if you need to make a presentation before community partners to invest, asking for commitments.

> *It's a long old road, but I know I'm gonna find the end.*
>
> – Bessie Smith

79) Read, study, and learn from other legacy builders.

Stay current on the justice news that fits your legacy goals. Learn about current trends, service failures or successes, legacy-building opportunities, new ideas and whatever information you can find. For example, if you have an excellent idea and a real passion for your future, read about the particular type of leaders that built legacies in history, strategy, and culture. This information will be a part of your legacy building plan.

> *Bringing the gifts that my ancestors gave, I am the dream*
> *and the hope of the enslaved. I rise. I rise. I rise.*
> – Maya Angelou

80) Be a scribe.

Have you ever had a justice service idea either through a dream, while doing the dishes, or sitting at your desk, and have thought that as soon as you have time, you will make a note of it. When that free time rolls around, you have forgotten some or all of these large ideas about your future. Keep a journal or notepad handy at all times. Smartphones now have an option that voice records and then transcribes. When you have an idea, get it down immediately, by any means necessary.

> *"I can't" are two words that have never been in*
> *my vocabulary. I believe in me more*
> *than anything in this world.*
> – Wilma Rudolph

81) Create a legacy plan.

Leaving a legacy is not about leaving something behind. It is about having an impact on others by utilizing your justice leadership skills. What do you want your legacy to be? Creating a legacy plan is your very first step if you are planning to build a sustained movement. This plan will be the blueprint for your success. The legacy plans will consist of philanthropic trends, financial planning, passion analysis, exit strategies, marketing and promotional options, everything about your future goals outside of just the service endeavor. The legacy plan answers the question "What is left when I am done?" A legacy plan allows you to keep track of everything involving your legacy goals.

Take responsibility for yourself, because no one's going to take responsibility for you. I'm not a victim. I grow from this, and I learn.

– Tyra Banks

82) How do you want to be remembered?

What do you want to be remembered for? Maybe you want to be remembered for your gracious and caring attitude, your ability to forge relationships, your passion. Keep how you want to be remembered in the forefront of your mind. How you treat people and manage your affairs while you are still here matters and can shape how people feel about your legacy. Some justice leaders have hopes of being remembered as selfless, or that their community work can continue to prosper without them there. Whatever is central to how you want to be remembered must be held onto and used as guiding principles as you build your legacy.

As a white person, I realized I had been taught about
racism as something that puts others at a disadvantage
but had been taught not to see one of its corollary aspects,
white skin privilege, which puts me at an advantage.

– Peggy McIntosh

83) Mentors matter.

Mentors have the opportunity to impact your life and legacy in profound ways. Maybe your mentors can help justice leaders with strategy decisions, so you feel confident when making choices. If you are looking for a mentor, there are many places to find them, such as justice elders in the community, or taking classes, or non-profit organizations, or faith groups. Make sure always to be thinking about how you can make legacy connections. If you don't have a mentor, you should. And if you're not mentoring someone, you should be.

You know, you do need mentors, but in the end, you just
need to believe in yourself.

—— Diana Ross

84) Family matters.

Your justice legacy is built from many parts of your life, friends, family, and business. Balance and family support play a huge part in creating your legacy.

If you don't understand yourself,
you don't understand anybody else.

— Nikki Giovanni

85) Who inspires you?

Is there somebody in your life that has influenced the fire within you? Sometimes the people who help us create the fire for our legacy are diverse and different. Revel in the power of diversity in experiences both personal and professional. It will make you a broader justice leader and person, and expand your idea of legacy. Diversity makes your life a lot more interesting. America is both an ideal and reality at the same time. We profess an ideal worthy of praise, but we must also contend with the fact that this ideal in a practical sense is out of reach for most. Your legacy and leadership should be about the promotion of a thriving justice, not a thin truth.

> I am not tragically colored. There is no great sorrow
> dammed up in my soul, nor lurking behind my eyes...
> Even in the helter-skelter skirmish that is my life, I
> have seen that the world is to the strong regardless of a
> little pigmentation more or less. No, I do not weep at the
> world—I am too busy sharpening my oyster knife.
>
> –Zora Neale Hurston

86) Destiny's child.

Sometimes a service endeavor saves us from having to work for anyone else and allows us to shape our future. Making the decisions on how best to steer your service into the future may be your only goal. However, when you can make your decisions about how best to operate, it is imperative that you take into account your long-term legacy. Part of creating your legacy means that you have some understanding of what is the first impression that people have of you and your company. First impressions happen way before people see you. Your impression representation always precedes you.

The moral arc of the universe bends
at the elbow of justice.
— Martin Luther King, Jr.

87) Giving and getting.

Do you love the idea of building your justice service endeavor and giving back to the community or communities in which you work to create change? By donating your time and resources, you build a relationship of mutuality, which is of particular importance these days. Become a conduit for good things and good works and your legacy will grow.

I'm for truth, no matter who tells it. I'm for justice,
no matter who it's for or against.
— Malcolm X

88) Inspire ambition in others.

You should strive to inspire ambition and hope in others. You must realize the impact you have on another's life, as well as your legacy. Sharing your justice leadership qualities in your community might motivate others to reach for something greater in themselves. It's important to be as authentic as possible. Try to be a good example for others. Be consistent with the mission and legacy you're trying to achieve.

Think like a queen. A queen is not afraid to fail. Failure
is another steppingstone to greatness.
— Oprah Winfrey

89) Living legacy.

You must change the way you conduct yourself so that you live that legacy. To live your legacy, you must be willing to examine behavioral changes, character development, education, working methods, relationship-building styles, etc. Monitoring and changing the way you live will allow you to be able to create the legacy you want to leave. Both your actions and words leave a legacy behind for others to follow. Make sure that you lead by example as well as by your words. Earlier generations will seek your wisdom and want to hear about your experiences. Share the lessons that have meant the most to you.

> *Charity is no substitute for justice. If we never challenge*
> *a social order that allows some to accumulate wealth—*
> *even if they decide to help the less fortunate—while*
> *others are short-changed, then even acts of kindness end*
> *up supporting unjust arrangements. We must never ignore*
> *the injustices that make charity necessary,*
> *or the inequalities that make it possible.*
> – Michael Eric Dyson

90) Legacy is about choices.

Some leaders leave financial legacies, supporting causes that mean the most to them. Other legacies are a positive institutional force in the community. These examples have their value, and all of them involve making choices about the type of legacy you want to leave.

> *I am a woman who came from the cotton fields of the*
> *South. From there I was promoted to the washtub. From*
> *there I was promoted to the cook kitchen. And from there*
> *I promoted myself into the business of manufacturing*
> *hair goods and preparations... I have built my own*
> *factory on my own ground.*
> – Madam C.J. Walker

91) Your legacy must come from within.

Deciding exactly what you want to put out into the world, look inward first. Focus on understanding your strengths and gifts. If you have difficulty with this, then talk to your colleagues, friends, and family members for their insight. Keep a running list, and see which strengths come up most frequently. Often, others see our gifts more clearly than we do. What are you passionate about and what do you find interesting? Many of us are drawn to settings, activities, and people that allow us to express ourselves. Make your legacy about the love of things, not a job to do.

But don't tell me [racism] is a figment of my imagination.
And when we grieve, don't tell us what to grieve for, and
don't tell us how long we should grieve. They don't tell
Jewish people that they should get over the Holocaust.
– Shannon Sharpe

92) Legacies change other people's circumstances.

Always remember that when it comes to changing others' circumstances, you can – you have that power. As an example, women who are in abusive situations often feel controlled and powerless to get out of the situation. What helps them often is one person who believes in them and their dreams. They have the choice of changing their circumstances, but everyone needs help sometimes. Your legacy is not about you but what it can help others do.

I grew up poor and white. While my class oppression has been relatively visible to me, my race privilege has not. In my efforts to uncover how race has shaped my life, I have gained deeper insight by placing race in the center of my analysis and asking how each of my other group locations has socialized me to collude with racism. In so doing, I have been able to address in greater depth my multiple locations and how they function together to hold racism in place. I now make the distinction that I grew up poor and white, for my experience of poverty would have been different had I not been white.

– DiAngelo, 2006

93) No shortcuts to a lasting legacy.

An old cliché states, "Anything worth doing is worth doing well." This should be your motto. When you want to succeed, you cannot afford to take shortcuts. Legacy shortcuts lead to imperfection and inadequacies. Always strive for the best, even if it requires a little more time and effort.

When there is no enemy within,
the enemies outside cannot hurt you.

– African Proverb

94) Seek and receive.

Whatever your idea of success, conduct a "legacy check" throughout the process of reaching your legacy goal. Do this with someone you trust and who is successful. Ask them to provide honest feedback about your success, and as you move through different milestones, bounce concerns or new ideas off them to help keep you on the right track in achieving a lasting legacy. Legacy checks can be brutal and enlightening as to you impressions and progress. Write down or record your feedback so that you may use it later for self-study.

*If I didn't define myself for myself, I would be crunched
into other people's fantasies for me and eaten alive.*

– Audre Lorde

95)   Birds of a feather.

If you have a goal of being the best justice leader you can be, then you will need to find friends and mentors who either have achieved that same or similar goal. It is important to surround yourself with people who can associate with your goal and passion; people who understand the burning desire to succeed and can encourage you when you meet with disappointments. This will also allow you to sample how others construct their legacies up close and develop community with each other.

*You are the designer of your destiny;
you are the author of your story.*

– Lisa Nichols

96)   An engine with no oil.

While being determined is important, do not be so hard on yourself that you become critical of every move you make. Give yourself some room to make mistakes and be flexible with self. That does not mean you can miss goals, but it does mean that if you do, you find out how to avoid that from happening again and then get back to business. Self-care and support systems are the oil in the legacy-building engine. Frequent and proper maintenance is a must.

*For Africa to me ... is more than a glamorous fact. It is
an historical truth. No man can know where he is going
unless he knows exactly where he has been and exactly
how he arrived at his present place.*

– Maya Angelou

97) Clean pain and dirty pain of legacy building.

We avoid the topic of legacy because we're uncomfortable with the notion of planning, which causes a much dirtier pain and has less capacity-building possibilities. As justice leaders, we are sometimes faced with a choice between clean pain and dirty pain. Clean is the pain of facing the things that we don't want to. Dirty pain is the pain of moving around self-confrontation. You will rarely be faced with the choice of No Pain and Pain. Building a legacy means choosing what road to travel. Each choice will shape your legacy.

Never underestimate the power of dreams and the influence of the human spirit. We are all the same in this notion: The potential for greatness lives within each of us.
– Wilma Rudolph

98) Manage time.

Being successful also means keeping to a schedule. Also, you need to learn how much is too much. Real-time and resource management will help you ensure that you use your time wisely and that you are not adding third portions onto a plate still overflowing with seconds. Learning to manage time rather than time managing you is one key to bringing balance to your legacy destiny.

Each person must live their life as a model for others.
– Rosa Parks

99) Power train.

The unconscious mind is a very powerful tool. Take advantage of this and each night before heading off to bed, take some time to pose legacy questions to yourself and then allow your mind to hash them out while you sleep. Also, meditate in whatever way you find relaxing before going to bed to clear your mind from clutter and allow the subconscious mind to go to work. When you go to bed before you fall asleep briefly say what you are hopeful for and let it marinate in your subconscious

The greatest gift is not being afraid to question.
– Ruby Dee

100) Keep recordings.

Always keep your records up-to-date. This would include contact information, legacy planning, community information, business plans, insurance, bills, attorney information, accounting, everything you touch regarding your legacy goal. Also, keep your files on your computer backed up in paper form and current. First, you never know when you are going to be asked for a particular document and need to provide quick turn-around. Second, computers do crash, and it would be a disaster if all of your information were suddenly gone.

Is solace anywhere more comforting than that
in the arms of a sister.
– Alice Walker

101) All work and no pay.
Challenge the ideas of the "go it alone justice leader" and working without balance.

Being successful means taking care of you, both physically and emotionally. You will need to have energy, focus, rest, and support of community. In turn, this will help you concentrate and put in the hours required to be successful. Without taking proper care of yourself, you will end up struggling, and your service to others could feel the effects. You need to be sure to allow yourself some time just for pleasure. Being successful is hard work, so to avoid burnout; you need to treat yourself to a night out or just time to sit back, read, watch TV, and do absolutely nothing once in a while. When you strive to be successful, stress is a natural part of the process. Do everything you can to avoid toxic stress. Adding in unnecessary stress into the equation will take focus away from accomplishing your goals. You can listen to relaxing tapes, get a professional massage, take a walk, or whatever helps you to relax. Being activated can tax the system; adding softer things to your life can help your body settle. When you start feeling overwhelmed, slow things way down, change direction, and avoid stress. The only thing toxic stress accomplishes is draining your think power and creativity. A toxic, stressed mentality constricts that energy needed to build a successful legacy.

> *I've learned that people will forget what you said,*
> *people will forget what you did, but people will never*
> *forget how you made them feel.*
> – Maya Angelou

SELF-STUDY QUESTIONS AND INSIGHTS

What are the top 10 legacy tips that stood out to you and why?

1)

2)

3)

4)

5)

6)

7)

8)

9)

10)

What insights did you get from the quotes in this section?

What did this section make you feel?

LAST WORD

When I think about justice, I'm reminded of the biblical parable and the account of the Good Samaritan. Luke 10:25-37, New International Version (NIV):

> On one occasion an expert in the law stood up to test Jesus. "Teacher," he asked, "what must I do to inherit eternal life?"
>
> "What is written in the Law?" he replied. "How do you read it?"
>
> He answered, "'Love the Lord your God with all your heart and with all your soul and with all your strength and with all your mind'; and, 'Love your neighbor as yourself.'"
>
> "You have answered correctly," Jesus replied. "Do this, and you will live."
>
> But he wanted to justify himself, so he asked Jesus, "And who is my neighbor?"
>
> In reply, Jesus said: "A man was going down from Jerusalem to Jericho when he was attacked by robbers. They stripped him of his clothes, beat him and went away, leaving him half dead. A priest happened to be going down the same road, and when he saw the man, he passed by on the other side. So too, a Levite, when he came to the place and saw him, passed by on the other side. But a Samaritan, as he traveled, came where the man was; and when he saw him, he took pity on him. He went to him and bandaged his wounds, pouring on oil and wine. Then he put the man on his donkey, brought him to an inn and took care of him. The next day he took out two denarii and gave them to the innkeeper. 'Look after him,' he said, 'and when I return, I will reimburse you for any extra expense you may have.'

"Which of these three do you think was a neighbor to the man who fell into the hands of robbers?"

The expert in the law replied, "The one who had mercy on him."

Jesus told him, "Go and do likewise."

As a veteran peace officer who takes great pride in the service to my community, I have come to the realization that real justice is not merely a system response to a grievance or wrong that has occurred, but rather the mercy that one human being unconditionally gives to another person.

In this book *Life, Leadership, and Legacy: 101 Tips for Emerging Justice Leaders* Mr. Menakem like the Good Samaritan unselfishly provides justice leaders with the tools they need to serve a purpose, inspiration, and love. Yes, we can use words to describe justice leaders like innovative, tireless, progressive, and forward thinkers, however, all justice leaders should have a love for their community just like the Good Samaritan had for his neighbor left on the side of the road. It is abundantly evident that Mr. Menakem not only loves his lifelong work in the areas of leadership and self-care, but he genuinely loves and respects the journey and dedication of emerging justice leaders.

If you serve others with love, mercy, and unselfishness, then I encourage you to read this book. If you struggle in service to others and want to learn ways to be a better servant leader, this book will not leave you on the side of the road. Mr. Menakem is a powerful, compelling, and inspirational messenger through his book.

– Medaria Arradondo
Deputy Chief-Chief of Staff
Minneapolis Police Department

NATIONAL SHOCK AND COMMUNAL CARE

As people in general and justice leaders precisely, we are going through a sort of national shock. It is my hope that this information is helpful for you in light of the election results and civil restlessness. I strongly encourage you to take some time to work on your shock. Here is some information about shock and guidelines for how you may be able to regulate some of it yourself:

Almost all of us are in a state of shock and startle in addition to outrage, sadness, fear, disgust, determination, and so on. There is a high level of activation involved in a shocking and startling experience. When shock charge is not worked through:

> We remain in a state of shock and are unable to orient and assess precisely what happened and is happening.
>
> Common expressions of disorientation include recurring and looping thoughts such as "I can't believe it! How could this happen!? Is this real!? How did I not see it coming!? Am I in a nightmare!?"
>
> Disorientation then leads to increase in activation and many manifest in panic, helpless rage, constant teariness, etc. It can also overwhelm the nervous system.
>
> Common expressions of overwhelming include the inability to focus, numbness, surrealness, despair, collapse, the impulse to isolate, an impulse to give up, horror, etc.

In the coming days and weeks and throughout Trump's presidency, we will no doubt continue to experience national shock time and again. To avoid the shock charge accumulating in your nervous system and negatively impacting your health, judgment, sense of self, and relationships, it is paramount that you work through the current shock charge.

I invite you to do the following:

> When you can, set aside some quiet time for yourself, sense your body as you think about President Trump.

> Focus your attention on sensations and felt sense rather than thoughts and emotions.

> You are likely to notice shock charge such as electric sensations, jolts, buzzing, twitches, etc. You may also notice your eyes and mouth wide open, hands wanting to cover your mouth or sides of your face, impulse to say/scream "No!", etc.; it is like the painting, "The Scream."

> Stay with these sensations and impulses, and they are likely to turn into discharge sensations such as tingling, trembling, chattering in the jaw, tears, heat/shivers, twitches, etc.

> Welcome, and allow the discharge to run its course.

> As the discharge settles, you may notice feeling lighter or more grounded, alertness and curiosity returning, hunger, desire to connect with nature, pets and people, outrage and determination to make a difference, etc. You may also experience spontaneous images of beauty, peace, and community, a sense of optimism, insights, etc.

> Take time to anchor these images, insights, feelings, sensations, and felt sense.

> Please note that, if you find yourself unable to stay focused and do the above or your experiences vary from the above, it is not the case that you are doing it incorrectly. You may need someone

or a healing community to guide you through the process because activation associated with bigotry and shock is often too high for any individual to be able to regulate themselves.

In times like this, it is important that we come together to support each other and develop community. People can regulate out of this initial post-election shock together.

– Thea Lee
Therapist/Community Practitioner,
Saint Paul/Minneapolis

IN THE SPIRIT JUST LEADING

A Pastor is someone who has spiritual care over a congregation. The word in Greek is *poimen* and means shepherd. Therefore, a pastor is a shepherd of God's flock who is to instruct, teach, and protect the people under his or her charge. John 10:10-15 states:

> *the thief comes only to steal and kill and destroy. I came that they may have and enjoy life, and have it in abundance [to the full, till it overflows]. I am the Good Shepherd. The Good Shepherd lays down His [own]life for the sheep.*

What does shepherding have to do with justice? I define justice as a broad notion that is based on a concept of moral rightness that incorporates varying perspectives on fairness, ethics, rationality, religion, and law. Which taps into my theory that we, as pastors, have to understand that first and foremost we are to lead people to salvation, and yet I believe that we are responsible for not just their salvation but systems that govern where we live. In being able to efficiently execute this, we must be culturally alert, not only to our community but all communities, paired with the heart of God.

In that, we will not be led by emotion, prejudices, theologies, philosophies, or norms that discount the mandate given by God, which is to love our neighbor as ourselves. A justice leader understands that his or her position is just a platform to carry the mandate of promoting rightness. Amos writes in 5:22-24:

> *Even though you bring me burnt offerings and grain offerings, I will not accept them. Though you bring choice fellowship offerings, I will have no regard for them. Away with the noise of your songs! I will not listen to the music of your harps. But let justice roll on like a river, righteousness like a never-failing stream.*

Religious activities without fairness and virtue is against what God requires of us. Moreover, the righteous and justice acts He demands are not the intermittent kind showing up here or there. But the constant kind that rolls down like waters and is an ever-flowing stream. It is imperative that we are not mere perpetrators, but those whose hearts are truly for the people.

The tendency to sit back and watch and say it's not my job to get involved in that is a cop out, and pastors must understand there is an obligation to speak truth to the powers that be. Speaking truth will be established by your ability to discern what God desires for you to address. The pastor must have the capacity to hear distinctly and be attuned to a cry imperceptible to others. In other words, we need to see and know things that would not ordinarily be seen or known by the average person; we are given this ability because of our relationship with Christ. An ordinary and standout theme of the book of Amos is God's destruction of Israel due to the injustice and hypocrisy of the wealthy and the ruling class. He also talked about how those practicing religious formalities were not handling the business of social justice.

Abraham Heschel, says in his book, *The Prophets*, "To us a single act of injustice – cheating in business, exploitation of the poor, is slight; to the prophets, a disaster. To us injustice is injurious to the welfare of the people; to the prophets, it is a death-blow to existence: to us, an episode; to them a catastrophe, a threat to the world." We must be able to put our life on the line like the good shepherd for our sheep and our community as we look out for the snares of injustice and be ready to speak and hold others accountable. We do this as our mandate to look upon our world through God's eyes in which all are precious in His sight, and he loves them so much. Racism, sexism, poverty, incarceration, and housing discrimination are waiting for you to leave the pulpit and get into the fight.

– Pastor Darrell Gillespie,
Proverbs Christian Fellowship

Bonus Tips and Quotes

We are all gifted. That is our inheritance.

– Ethel Waters

GET YOUR REPS UP

Reputation as an emerging justice leader is usually built on three things: Consistency, perseverance and open attitude. The bottom line is that your reputation is constructed from cultivating exceptional relationship and consistent behavior. Consistency, perseverance and attitude have been seen as something you have or you don't. In reality, consistency can be taught. Consistency is skill and like with any skill it takes repetition. Over time the reps help you understand the nuance of the consistency skill and that helps to build confidence. The fear that comes with learning anything new can become fuel for transformation rather than a barrier.

You're not obligated to win. You're obligated to keep trying to do the best you can every day.

– Marian Wright Edelman

BE HUMBLE

Being a justice leader is hard and complicated. Many justice leaders get caught in trying to be good at every facet of their service to others. The reality is that there are so many people out there who are smarter and stronger than you in certain key areas. Partner with people that are strong in areas where you are weaker. If you are a visionary justice leader but struggle with the organization then partner with individuals that come naturally too. This means that you must put your pride aside and listen and learn.

We never know how our small activities will affect others through the invisible fabric of our connectedness. In this exquisitely connected world, it's never a question of "critical mass." It's always about critical connections.

– Grace Lee Boggs

I have learned over the years that when one's mind is made up, this diminishes fear; knowing what must be done does away with fear.

– Rosa Parks

I am a feminist, and what that means to me is much the same as the meaning of the fact that I am Black: it means that I must undertake to love myself and to respect myself as though my very life depends upon self-love and self-respect.

– June Jordan

It's not the load that breaks you down; it's the way you carry it.

– Lena Horne

The triumph can't be had without the struggle.
                                    – Wilma Rudolph

Success doesn't come to you ... you go to it.
                                    – Marva Collins

Surround yourself with only people who are
going to lift you higher.
                                    – Oprah Winfrey

Everything will change. The only question is
growing up or decaying.
                                    – Nikki Giovanni

Whether you come from a council estate or a country
estate, your success will be determined
by your own confidence and fortitude.
                                    – Michelle Obama

A crown, if it hurts us, is not worth wearing.
                                    – Pearl Bailey

If I didn't define myself for myself, I would be crunched
into other people's fantasies for me and eaten alive.
                                    – Audre Lorde

I have found that among its other benefits,
giving liberates the soul of the giver.
– Maya Angelou

Think like a queen. A queen is not afraid to fail.
Failure is another steppingstone to greatness.
– Oprah Winfrey

When I dare to be powerful – to use my strength in
the service of my vision, then it becomes less and less
important whether I am afraid.
– Audre Lorde

The triumph can't be had without the struggle.
– Wilma Rudolph

Trust yourself. Think for yourself. Act for yourself. Speak
for yourself. Be yourself. Imitation is suicide.
– Marva Collins

Justice Leadership Planning Questions

No person is your friend who demands your silence or denies your right to grow.

— Alice Walker

- What is it that makes you unique?

- What are the dreams that never left you?

- How would you rekindle the fire in those dreams?

- What would a timeline look like?

- What are the ways that you nurture collective justice processes?

- In what ways do you participate in communal care procedures?

- In what ways are your communal infrastructure development ideas sustainable?

- Do you still believe that your work matters?

- What was the first hurt you felt in doing justice work?

- What is the worst thing about your job?
- In what ways do you co-create community with others?
- How has stress impacted your life and leadership capacities?
- What do you want to be known for?
- What gets in the way providing justice leadership?
- What are the daily self-care routines that you employ?
- What self-care practices do you employ after civil restlessness?

Answer these questions on a separate piece of paper and review after

Don't wait around for other people to be happy for you.
Any happiness you get you've got to make yourself.
— Alice Walker

Justice Leadership Solutions

Coaching the Courageous Few through Struggle and Strife

Justice Leadership Coaching and Training

Are you a justice leader on the front lines of change? You still believe in justice for all people and want to take your current organization to the next level—all while building a more balanced life, and creating a legacy you can be proud of.

Have you ever felt that...

- You have you become cynical or critical at work?

- The job has changed for the worst?

- You've become disillusioned, frustrated, and exhausted?

- The fire that you came with to make a difference has burned out?

- You are unappreciated for the work you do?

- You lack satisfaction from your achievements?

If you answered yes to any of these questions, then your next step is to partner with Justice Leadership Solutions (JLS).

Trainings and Offerings

Aspirational Coaching and Training

Justice leadership coaching partners with you to find your own answers. No cookie cutter blueprint to follow; instead, Resmaa Menakem partners with you so that you discover your unique justice vision and intelligence through structure, accountability, and guidance. If you are a justice leader who needs a partner and structure to push that fire that burns inside of you to brighten paths rather burn them, then Resmaa Menakem is the justice coach for you.

Justice Leadership Solutions provides clients with strategic, firm, knowledgeable, and supportive mindful leadership coaching interactions for emerging justice leaders. The three focus areas of justice leadership coaching and training are:

- Nurturing a life in which success as a justice leader innovator and self-care complement one another

- Mindfully building and leading justice organizations that reflect the best of who you are

- Creating a lasting legacy of justice, service, and prosperity

Justice Life Coaching

Justice leaders face many obstacles when pushing for change. The pushing, in order to create change, can take a toll and be burdensome to justice leaders' lives. Many well-meaning justice leaders lose people and possessions close to them when they perform their justice leadership work. Balance is the key to being successful in life and in becoming an effective justice leader. It is for this reason that Justice Leadership Solutions partners with you to create a balanced life plan that allows for swift adaption to changes. JLS does this by offering **twelve dynamic individual phone coaching and accountability sessions.**

Justice Leadership Coaching

For justice leaders, having a world-changing idea isn't enough. Being a leader means understanding leadership principles and the ability to influence others in those same principles. It means understanding your struggles and strife and their importance as you develop your unique justice vision and skill sets. JLS encourages and provokes you to bring forth those leadership qualities that have been thwarted by offering **twenty-four spectacular individual phone coaching and accountability sessions.**

Organizational Justice Strategy Coaching

Being a justice leader in an established organization can be a daunting proposition. Attempting to balance organizational values and responsibilities with your own life and justice values can stretch the strongest and most directed person. JLS has the organizational expertise and understands these demands. JLS supports and inspires you in developing organizational qualities that are important in taking your justice vision to a new reality by offering **thirty-six spectacular individual phone coaching and accountability sessions.**

Training Service Offerings

Justice Leadership Solution's creation of FyrePush.com, an online web portal exclusively for justice leaders, takes your learning to new heights with its powerful organizational and wellness tools. The customized in-person and web-based leadership workshops provide navigation in the dynamics of race, organizational inclusion, and matters of de-escalation. Psychological & mental health first aid certificates, group coaching, and passionate speaking engagements for teams can be accessed and made available by request. JLS's unique concept provokes you into bringing forth those leadership qualities that have been thwarted in the past. Take advantage of JLS's isolated strategy and consultation services by request. You have strong commitment and values that make a difference. Resmaa Menakem of Justice Leadership Solutions is here, to partner with you and to breathe life into your justice work.

You have strong beliefs, and value making a difference. Resmaa Menakem of Justice Leadership Solutions is here to partner with you to breathe more life into your justice work.

Resmaa Menakem is a visionary justice leadership coach, organizational strategist, and master trainer. Resmaa is the premiere dynamic justice leadership coach who is dedicated to partnering with you so your dreams become your reality. Resmaa is passionate about coaching those courageous leaders that dedicate their lives toward making the world a better place. If you want a remarkably bright future, then Resmaa Menakem is the justice leadership coach for you.

Contact Resmaa today
for pricing information
612-810-2605
www.justiceleadershipsolutions.net
RESMAA@JUSTICELEADERSHIPSOLUTIONS.NET

7400 Metro Blvd., Suite 224
Edina, Minnesota 55439

Author's Story

*I freed a thousand of the enslaved. I could have freed a
thousand more if only they knew they were enslaved.*
— Harriet Tubman

Resmaa Menakem is a visionary justice leadership coach,
organizational strategist, and master trainer. He is a dynamic
and fully engaged justice leadership coach who is dedicated to
partnering with leaders whose intention is to assist others in
leading better lives. Resmaa is passionate about coaching those
courageous leaders who dedicate their lives toward making the
world a better place.

Resmaa Menakem is the founder of Justice Leadership
Solutions, a Justice Leadership consultancy firm dedicated to
"coaching leaders through civil unrest and restlessness; justice
leaders who feel isolated; and for those who sense that their
voice is unsupported and feels somewhat cynical, but who still
have the fire and desire for change and creating justice for all."
Resmaa is an accomplished author of three compelling books;
101 Tips for Emerging Justice Leaders, a book on conflict in relationships titled *Rock the Boat: How to use Conflict to Heal and Deepen Relationships,* and *My Grandmothers Hands: Racialized Trauma and the
Patterns to Mending Our Bodies and Hearts.*

As a prodigious public speaker, radio and television per-
sonality, Resmaa has appeared on *Oprah Winfrey* and *Dr. Phil* as
an expert on conflict mediation, self-care, and healing.

Resmaa has been a non-profit executive and business

owner for over 25 years. He possesses vast expert experience in strategic planning, equity leadership coaching, and marketing. Visit him at JusticeLeadershipsolutions.com.

Resmaa successfully coaches and trains a diversified array of justice leaders who are community activists, police leaders (administrative/management/community policing agents), clergy, and non-profit executives in achieving their objectives of change and justice, while partnering with them in making meaningful work experiences, as well as accomplishing life and career balance.

As an impressively experienced international trainer and skilled, effective communicator among diverse ethnic populations, Resmaa has instructed and trained personnel extensively in the UAE (United Arab Emirates) police departments, as well as provided years of experience as a Trauma Counselor and trainer to military and US contractors in Afghanistan.

Co-author's Story

A woman's gifts will make room for her.
                                                            – Hattie McDaniel

June Davidson, Ph.D., President of American Seminar Leaders Association and Coaching Firm International, completed advanced coaching studies at Harvard University and teaches nationally and internationally, including at the University of Bucharest. She is an authority on developing curriculum for higher education and corporate training. Dr. Davidson developed the ATAP method (Accessing Your Truth to Accelerate Your Process) using a brain pattern interrupt. Her trained coaches, corporate training, and seminar leaders are recognized worldwide and are licensed to use her method. She is a brilliant visionary and is dedicated to the stellar success of those she trains.

Acknowledgments

*We must not, in trying to think about how we can make a
big difference, ignore the small daily differences we can make
which, over time, add up to big differences
that we often cannot foresee.*
— Marian Wright Edelman

In the beginning, there was the blackness, not nothingness, but the blackness. In the blackness is that state of potential. This book acknowledges that potential and the import of developing a transformational collective infrastructure that sets the stages for sustainable communal development. This book is dedicated to all of the justice leader ancestors, many of whom are quoted and referenced in this book, who created a way out of nothingness with blood, bone, and body. This book is dedicated to the elders that taught, protected, and died so that we may experience somethingness rather than nothingness.

This book is devoted to the current and future justice leaders, regardless of vocation, paving the way with their intelligence, tenacity, and their feet. This book is dedicated to promoting more self and communal affirmation, more self-care, more softness, and more self-love for emerging justice leaders.

In this book, self-care is defined by restoration and reclamation, which are hallmarks for balanced life for justice leaders. Justice leaders have a long history in pushing for change, with much of it being practiced in the context of community.

I want to thank Coaching Firm International, My beautiful family and my community for giving solace and support.

CPSIA information can be obtained
at www.ICGtesting.com
Printed in the USA
LVHW011058150720
660705LV00004B/289

9 780998 424828